To tortoises everywhere

Published in the United States in 1999 by
The Millbrook Press, Inc.,
2 Old New Milford Road, Brookfield, CT 06804

Designed and produced by The Templar Company plc
Pippbrook Mill, London Road, Dorking, Surrey RH4 1JE, Great Britain

Edited by AJ Wood
Additional design by Mike Jolley

This book was drawn in ink and painted in watercolor and gouache on watercolor paper.
It was set in 25pt Bernhard Modern.

Library of Congress Cataloging-in-Publication Data:
Ward, Helen, 1962–
The hare and the tortoise : a fable from Aesop / retold & illustrated by Helen Ward.
p.   c.m.
Summary: Retells the events of the famous race between the boastful hare and the persevering tortoise.
ISBN 0-7613-1318-4 (lib.bdg.)   0-7613-0988-8 (tr. bdg.)
[1. Fables. 2. Folklore.] I. Aesop. II. Hare and the tortoise. English. III. Title.
PZ8.2.W285 Har   398.24'52792—dc21
[E]   98-26100
CIP
AC

Printed in Belgium

3 5 4 2 (lib. bdg.)   3 5 4 2 (tr. bdg.)

THE

HARE *and* *the* TORTOISE

A Fable from Aesop

Retold & Illustrated by

HELEN WARD

THE MILLBROOK PRESS

Brookfield, Connecticut

There once was a very fast hare...

and a very slow tortoise.

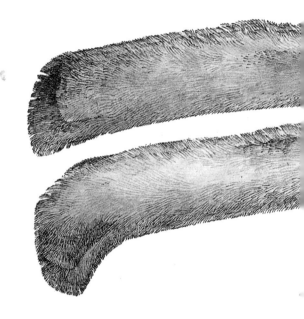

The hare hurtled everywhere causing havoc.

The tortoise
was an altogether more
thoughtful animal.

One day the hare was carelessly sprinting along
when he tripped over the tortoise and
tumbled into a thorny bush…

which hurt.

The hare shouted at the tortoise.
The noise attracted a crowd.

The hare called the tortoise slow-witted and stupid.
The tortoise did not say what he
thought of the hare.

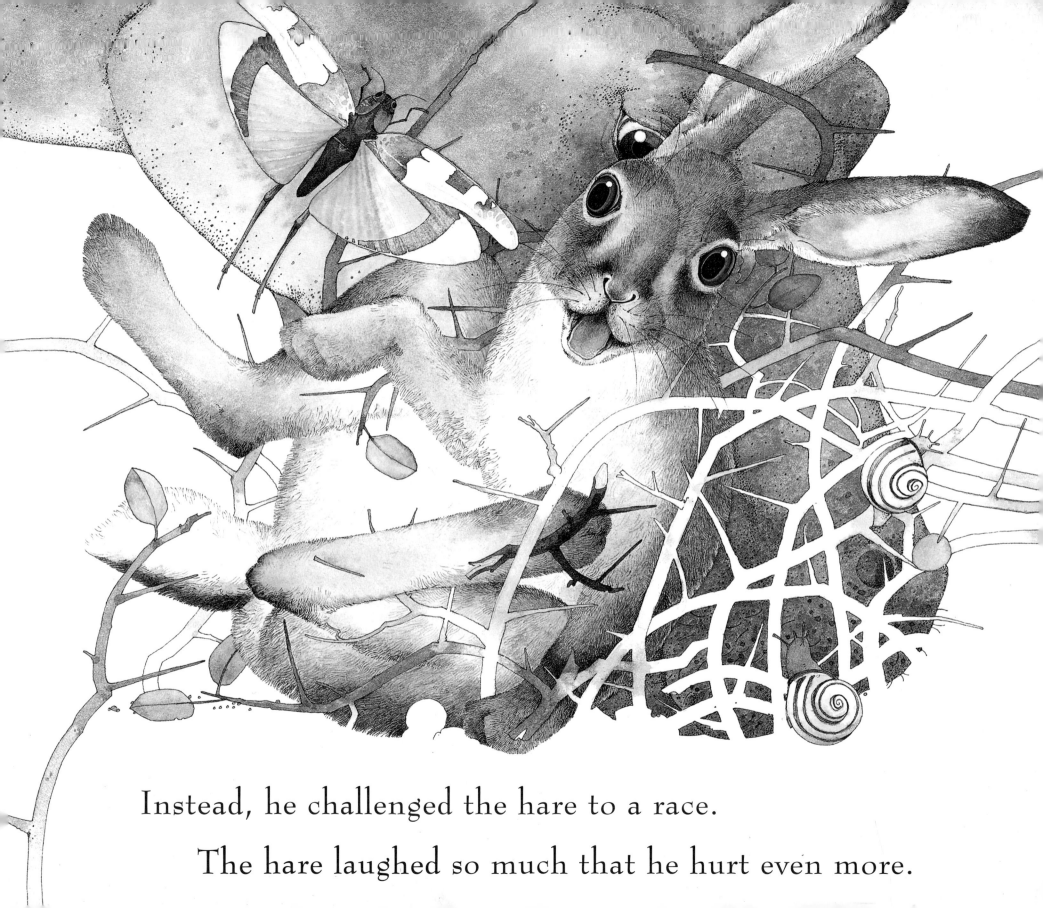

Instead, he challenged the hare to a race.

The hare laughed so much that he hurt even more.

News of the challenge spread far and wide.

From all corners of the Earth an audience began to gather.

A course was marked out...

An unbiased referee was found. At last the great day arrived!

The referee said,

   " On your marks... get set... GO!"

The hare hurtled forward

   in a leap and a bound,

   and was gone.

The tortoise plodded along,
    slowly and steadily, one foot after the other.

            He was soon left far behind.

The hare raced to
the river and
leaped...

from stone...

to stone...

toward the far bank...

...but he did not quite get to where he thought he was going.

The tortoise crossed more easily.

Next, the hare found himself in the thick of a very peculiar forest.

He was scratched and tired when he
reached the other side.

So the hare decided to take a nap...

After all, it was obviously going to take the tortoise
a very long time indeed to scramble through
those trees...

The hare woke to find himself in a vegetable garden.
He looked around and was pleased to see that the
tortoise was so far behind he was out of sight.
So the hare had plenty of time for a long lunch.

Or so he thought...

Halfway through his third helping, the hare was surprised to hear the sound of cheering.

He suddenly had a nasty feeling he knew what the cheering was for. Horrified, he ran as fast as a hare with a long lunch inside him could run.

Not fast enough! The patient, plodding tortoise

had beaten him to the finish line.

But although the hare was not fast enough

to win the race,

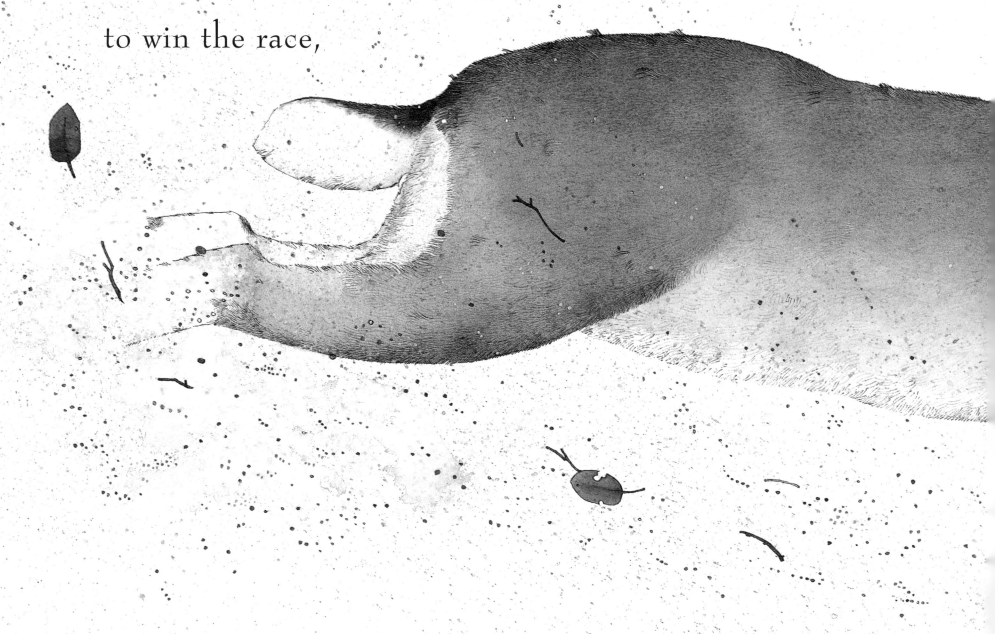

he was running too fast to stop.

He fell into an even thornier bush than before...

But this time

he said nothing.

KEY TO THE
ANIMALS

There Was Once a Very Fast Hare …
All species of hares are fast runners, thanks to their long hind legs and strong leg muscles. The common brown hare *(Lepus capensis),* pictured throughout this book, is found in many parts of the world. It was introduced into North and South America, Australia, and New Zealand from its original home in Europe so that it could be hunted for food and sport. Unlike many other small mammals, it does not burrow, but relies on its speed and vigilance to escape danger. Just as well, then, that grown male hares can reach speeds of up to 43 miles (70 kilometers) per hour — faster than the world's fastest racehorse!

… and a Very Slow Tortoise
Although not the slowest creatures in the world, tortoises have a long-standing reputation for slowness. Most move at speeds of around only 1,180 feet (360 meters) per hour — in other words, it would take over four hours for

our hero to travel a mile! The belief that tortoises hardly move at all is not helped by the fact that, when threatened, they will not try to flee like most other animals. Instead, a frightened tortoise will stay perfectly still, retracting its head and feet beneath its armored shell, in hopes that this will provide sufficient protection from its enemies. The tortoise featured throughout this book is known as Hermann's tortoise *(Testudo hermanni),* the species most commonly found in pet stores.

Causing Havoc
None of these creatures is speedy enough to get out of the way of a hurrying hare. In the case of the edible snail, that's hardly surprising since it is one of the world's slowest creatures, taking an hour to move only 15 feet (4.5 meters). From left to right you can see an ocellated lizard, cockchafer (Junebug), garden dormouse, and quail, as well as the Roman, or edible, snail.

An Altogether More Thoughtful Animal
How thoughtful of the tortoise to provide this dwarf mongoose with a look-out post! The mongoose is a speedy snake catcher, often kept as a pet in its original home of Asia.

The Noise Attracted a Crowd
Aside from the hare and the tortoise, the gathering crowd shows, from left to right, the dwarf mongoose, common chameleon, European quail, fennec fox, impala, short-horned grasshopper, and a banded snail.

From All Corners of the Earth … (far left)
Among the animals that have gathered from far and wide you can see the world's fastest flying bird, the peregrine falcon. This impressive bird of prey will dive through the sky at speeds reaching 80 miles (131 kilometers) per hour or more, knocking its prey of other smaller birds to the

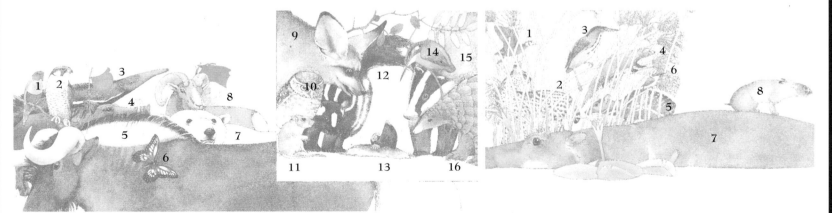

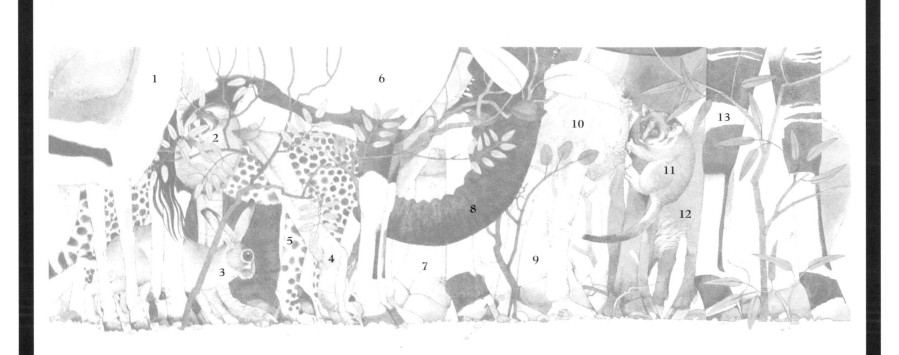

ground with a single blow of its sharp talons! At the opposite end of the scale, you can also see the dusky swallowtail butterfly, which has the slowest wing beat in the insect world at 300 beats per minute!

1. Rainbow lory
2. Peregrine falcon
3. Giant anteater
4. African warthog
5. White-tailed gnu
6. Dusky swallowtail butterfly
7. Polar bear
8. American bighorn sheep
9. Bat-eared fox
10. Burrowing owl
11. African gerbil
12. Spotted skunk
13. European mole
14. Kingfisher
15. Eurasian badger
16. Pangolin

But He Did Not Quite Get To Where He Thought He Was Going (previous page, right)

Like the tortoise, the hippopotamus has a reputation for being slow and lazy. True, hippos do spend practically all day resting but they can actually move quite quickly if they want to, especially when running along the river bottom. However, they are most often found standing up to their necks in river water or reed beds where they can sleep unobserved, with only their eyes and nostrils poking up above the surface.

The group of waterside dwellers also includes:

1. Pygmy goose
2. Serval
3. Green heron
4. Egyptain mongoose
5. Water chevrotain
6. White-collared kingfisher
7. Hippopotamus
8. Hare

A Very Peculiar Forest (above)

Among this fine array of legs are those belonging to some of the speediest creatures on Earth.

The cheetah is the fastest mammal on land and can reach speeds of over 60 miles (100 kilometers) per hour when chasing its prey across the African plains. It shares its home with the world's fastest land bird — the ostrich. With its powerful legs, flexible knees, and two-toed feet, the ostrich is capable of reaching 45 miles (72 kilometers) per hour — fast enough to outrun most of its enemies, which is just as well since it is too big to fly! Most of the other animals shown are also quick on their feet except, of course, for the slow loris, who, as its name implies, spends most of its life climbing slowly through the branches of its forest home.

1. Thomson's gazelle
2. Slow loris
3. Hare
4. Ostrich
5. Cheetah
6. Oryx
7. Indian rhinoceros
8. African elephant
9. Giraffe
10. Vicuña
11. Common ringtail
12. Red river hog
13. Okapi

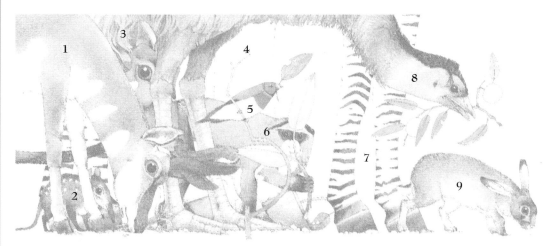

When He Reached the Other Side (above)

Continuing through the forest of legs you can see:

1. Pronghorn antelope   2. Giant elephant shrew
3. Bongo   4. Giraffe
5. Gouldian finch   6. De Brazza's monkey
7. Zebra   8. Emu
9. And, of course, a very tired hare!

Plenty of Time For a Long Lunch …

Did you spot the chinchilla (top) and northern grasshopper mouse (bottom) hiding among the vegetables? Both are used to living in the most inhospitable climates — the grasshopper mouse in the hot, dry deserts of the American Southwest, the chinchilla in the cold, rocky mountains of Bolivia and Chile.

The Sound of Cheering (right)

And so we reach the end of the race! You might have expected the cheetah to have gotten there before the hare — after all, he is the fastest creature on Earth, but somehow even the world's slowest animals have managed to make it to the finish line as well! The three-toed sloth holds the record for being the slowest mammal, crawling along on the ground at a mere 518 feet (158 meters) per hour. It would take the sloth about ten hours to travel a mile. In fact, this animal spends so much time staying still that microscopic algae actually grow on its fur. However, even the sloth is faster than the red slug, who would take more than four weeks to travel that same mile!

1. Roadrunner — third-fastest land bird after the ostrich and emu, running at 26 miles (42 kilometers) per hour.
2. Armadillo — although capable of moving quite quickly, the nine-banded armadillo holds the record for being one of sleepiest animals on Earth, spending 80 percent of its life fast asleep!
3. Cheetah — fastest land mammal at 70 miles (115 kilometers) per hour.
4. Arctic Tern — holds the record for the longest flight of any bird at 16,000 miles (26,000 kilometers).
5. Black buck — third-fastest land mammal after the cheetah and pronghorn antelope, running at 50 miles (80 kilometers) per hour.
6. Camel — at 10 miles (16 kilometers) per hour, one of the fastest animals in the desert.

7. Long-tailed hummingbird — the fastest wing beats in the bird world, some species can reach 90 beats a second.
8. European mole — a champion digger, the mole can dig over 65 feet (20 meters) in a single day.
9. Giraffe — with the longest legs in the animal kingdom, the giraffe can run at 30 miles (50 kilometers) per hour.
10. Monarch butterfly — makes the longest journey of any insect at 2.130 miles (3,400 kilometers).
11. Kangaroo — this marsupial can jump about 13 feet, (4 meters) in a single giant jump and reach a speed of 28 miles (45 kilometers) per hour.
12. Banded snail — Although faster than the edible snail, the banded variety would still take about a week and a half to travel a single mile!
13. Three-toed sloth — the world's slowest mammal, moving at only 518 feet (160 meters) per hour.
14. Gentoo penguin — the fastest swimmer in the bird world, with a top speed of 17 miles (27 kilometers) per hour.
15. Red slug — the world's slowest creature at 6 feet (2 meters) per hour.
16. And, to finish, who else but the slow and steady Hermann's tortoise!

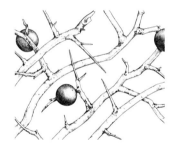